I0814489

To:

From:

Date:

Published in 2026
by Gemini Gift Books
Part of Gemini Books Group

Based in Woodbridge and London

Marine House, Tide Mill Way,
Woodbridge, Suffolk IP12 1AP
United Kingdom

www.geminibooks.com

Part of the Gemini Pockets series

Text by Becky Freeth
Cover illustration and internal graphics:
Shutterstock/littleWhale

ISBN 978-1-80247-413-8

A CIP catalogue record for this book is available from the British Library.

Manufacturer's EU Representative: Eurolink Compliance Limited, 25 Herbert Place, Dublin, D02 AY86, Republic of Ireland. admin@eurolink-europe.ie

Printed in China

10 9 8 7 6 5 4 3 2 1

THE POCKET

To the one I love

G:

Contents

INTRODUCTION

Love can strike in as little as four minutes. It will bowl you over, build you up and break you back down. But love is life – it's what makes us humans, and it's what makes life rich.

It doesn't have to be about romance, either. Love shows up in family, friendship, community – even in the way you care for yourself. All of it matters. All of it counts.

Love doesn't just move us emotionally – it changes us physically. Our brains react to it with flushed cheeks, sweaty palms and racing hearts. Sometimes, even talking about love can leave you feeling warm and fuzzy.

Joyfully, this little tome is dedicated to this big, messy beautiful thing we call love. So, go ahead – read on to your heart's content!

Chapter One

Love, Love, Love

Three Little Words

The word "love" traces back to the Sanskrit word *lubhyati*, meaning "desire".

The phrase "I love you" predates even Shakespeare – the bard often credited as love's most poetic storyteller. Long before the swooning sonnets of the nineteenth century, lovers in earlier eras would declare their affection with the timeless phrase: "I love thee."

Expressions of love are even found in ancient Egypt. The Egyptians wrote expressions of love that resembled those all-important three little words in songs and poems sent to the tombs with them. In fact, theorists believe it's one of the oldest feelings to exist, shaping our behaviour since the dawn of civilization.

Types of Love

The ancient Greeks believed that love came in many forms – some of which don't include desire at all.

From the kindness we show ourselves (the foundation for loving others) to the deep, unconditional bond between a parent and child, love was seen as complex, layered and essential to human life.

In their view, love wasn't just romance – it was friendship, self-respect, affection and deep devotion and loyalty.

Truly, love is a many-splendored thing.

1 Eros
Sexual Passion

Qualities:

Exciting, instinctive, intense

"Eros" is a fundamental form of love that comes from our survival instincts. It's the passion, lust and pleasure for another person, motivated by our primal need to procreate. The Greeks thought it was dangerous, fearing these instincts to be so intense that they could be "maddening".

2 Philia
Deep Friendship

Qualities:

Mutual, authentic, trustworthy

A platonic "Philia" love is a two-way friendship. While friendship is a pillar of all long-term relationships, this type of love is affection in the absence of attraction. It's a connection founded on shared goodwill and loyalty – the kind of love that ebbs and flows through our lives, making them more fulfilling.

3 Ludus
Playful Love

Qualities:

Thrilling, uncomplicated, non-exclusive

In today's society, "Ludus" would be similar to dating with "no strings attached". This could manifest as either a fleeting or a long-lasting connection, but it's based on a mutual and mature understanding that as long as you keep things casual, everyone has fun and nobody gets hurt.

4 Philautia
Love of the Self

Qualities:

Rewarding, constructive, compassionate

Oscar Wilde once said that "to love oneself is the beginning of a lifelong romance." His approach to love, like much of his work, was influenced by Aristotle, the Greek thinker who believed selfishness could be both positive and negative. The good (or noble) type prioritizes your own wellbeing enough for you to flourish in life.

5 Storge
Family Love

Qualities:

Unconditional, familiar, dependable

People describe a "mother's love" like an unstoppable force. A powerful, self-sacrificing, deep devotion. The ancient Greeks used the word "Storge" to describe this immeasurable love and dependence within families, which exists naturally between parent and child, siblings and grandparents.

6 Agape
Love for All Humanity

Qualities:

Unselfish, fulfilling, spiritual

"Agape" is the kind of love that expects nothing in return. It's a selfless devotion to others: a deep sense of compassion that values humanity as a whole. This kind of love puts the needs of others before your own, not out of duty, but out of genuine care. In today's world, we might understand this as helping strangers, standing up for justice or caring for the planet with future generations in mind. It's love at its most generous and inclusive.

7 Pragma
Longstanding Love

Qualities:

Faithful, mutually beneficial, consistent

Modern psychologists say "Pragma" is less about "falling in love" and more about "standing" in it – like a mutual agreement to love and be loved, bypassing, or outgrowing, the thrill and romance. Like a marriage, it's a longstanding commitment that is built on compromise, loyalty and a shared commitment to making the relationship work.

“I would rather spend one life-time with you, than face all the ages of this world alone.”

J.R.R. TOLKIEN,
THE LORD OF THE RINGS, 1954

"I Love You" in 6 languages

French: Je t'aime

Spanish: Te amo

Italian: Ti amo

German: Ich liebe dich

Portuguese: Eu te amo

Danish: Jeg elsker dig

Love Is Love

Love comes in all shapes, sizes and rainbow colours. The LGBTQ+ community reflects the full spectrum of what love can be – bold, tender, messy, magical and unapologetically real.

It's about the freedom to love openly, to be seen and celebrated and to shout it from the rooftops – no matter who you love, or how you love.

Plato-nic

Unlike the other Greek love labels, the concept of a "platonic" relationship has outlived the philosopher Plato, who helped coin the phrase about a type of love that doesn't involve sex.

These modern-day examples often co-exist with our romantic relationships:

Bromance: A brotherly love between men that is rooted in affection, not attraction.

Sisterhood: Steady and non-judgemental friendships between women built on trust and emotional honesty, sometimes including non-sexual physical touch.

Roommates: Sharing everything except a bedroom can build a rare kind of closeness – intimate, supportive and friendly.

I am not yours, not lost in you,
Not lost, although I long to be
Lost as a candle lit at noon,
Lost as a snowflake in the sea.

You love me, and I find you still
A spirit beautiful and bright,
Yet I am I, who long to be
Lost as a light is lost in light.

Oh plunge me deep in love – put out
My senses, leave me deaf and blind,
Swept by the tempest of your love,
A taper in a rushing wind.

SARA TEASDALE,
'I AM NOT YOURS', 1915

14 February

A day for the lovers, Valentine's Day is an annual celebration marked by cards, hearts, romantic dinners and sometimes even marriage proposals.

Its roots trace back to the third century and the saint who gave the day its name. St Valentine is remembered for defying the orders of Roman Emperor Claudius II by secretly marrying couples who were in love. The emperor believed that romantic relationships weakened his soldiers, and he banned marriages to keep them focused on war.

But for Valentine, love was worth the risk. He continued to perform weddings in secret, and for that, he was sentenced to death – on 14 February.

Valentine's Cards: *Sent With Love*

After St Valentine's death, couples began exchanging romantic notes in his honour – small tokens to commemorate his brave stand for love. But it wasn't until the nineteenth century, during the reign of Queen Victoria, that the tradition truly took off.

Today, an estimated one billion cards are sent each year around the world – making it the second-most popular card-sending occasion after Christmas. Whether handwritten or store-bought, the message remains the same: love is worth celebrating.

Valentine's Day: Five Facts

1. In the UK, men spend the most money on Valentine's Day but women are more likely to send cards than men.

2. South Koreans celebrate a romantic holiday on the 14th of every month, from Diary Day in January and Valentine's Day in February to Kiss Day in June.

3. In Finland and Estonia, 14 February is known as Friend's Day – a time to honour friendships with small gifts, cards or kind gestures.

4. In the US, it's estimated that around 220,000 marriage proposals take place on Valentine's Day.

5. In Japan, women usually give chocolates to men on Valentine's Day. The gesture is returned on White Day in March.

25 January

Dydd Santes Dwynwen (Wales)

Cards, gifts and Welsh love spoons are exchanged in celebration of the Welsh patron saint of lovers, Saint Dwynwen.

13 February

Galentine's Day (global)

A phrase coined in the early 2010s to celebrate the joy of female friendship.

29 August

Qixi Festival (China)

A traditional romantic festival for over 2,000 years.

12 June

Dia dos Namorados (Brazil)

A big feast and party that literally means "The Day of The Enamoured".

Pride

The ultimate celebration of love, Pride, takes place around the world throughout the month of June.

Loud, proud, confetti-covered and rainbow-coloured, the event not only promotes diversity of identity (and the importance of loving ourselves), but equality for lesbian, gay and bisexual relationships, celebrating love in all its forms.

"Love, the beauty of it, the joy of it and yes, even the pain of it, is the most incredible gift to give and to receive as a human being. And we deserve to experience love fully, equally, without shame and without compromise."

ACTOR AND TRANS ACTIVIST ELLIOT PAGE,
TIME TO THRIVE CONFERENCE,
14 FEBRUARY 2014

Love at First Sight

Only half of us believe you can fall in love with someone the first time you meet them. The other half have to see it to believe it.

In 1997, psychologist Professor Arthur Aron devised a series of 36 open-ended questions to help strangers fall in love in as little as four minutes. Deep, intimate, exposing questions like: What is your most treasured memory? How do you feel about your relationship with your mother?

The powerful act of staring into each other's eyes for four minutes afterwards intensified the experience, to the point where participants reported feeling "strongly attracted" to each other. One couple even went on to marry!

88 days

is the typical time between the first date and a declaration of love from a man.

134 days

is the typical time between the first date and a declaration of love from a woman.

180 days

is the typical time between the first date and a declaration of love in a lesbian relationship.

What Does Love Feel Like?

We used to believe that the fluttery feeling of falling in love came from our hearts. But science now tells us that it all starts in the brain – it's actually the result of a complex cocktail of seven key hormones, each playing a role in how we feel, bond and behave when we're in love.

Oxytocin: Often called the "love hormone", oxytocin is released during physical touch and intimacy. It's especially linked to long-term attachment – like the connection between a mother and her baby.

Vasopressin: This hormone contributes to feelings of closeness and commitment – but it also plays a part in jealousy and possessiveness.

Dopamine: The brain's "reward chemical", dopamine floods our system during moments of pleasure, making love feel exciting, addictive and euphoric.

Cortisol: Surprisingly, cortisol – the body's stress hormone – increases during the early stages of love, which explains why falling for someone can feel thrilling and anxiety-inducing.

Testosterone: Along with estrogen, these "sex hormones" drive physical attraction and desire. Dopamine then rewards the actions they inspire.

Serotonin: The chemical neurotransmitter serotonin, which helps regulate mood, actually drops during early stages of attraction – possibly explaining the sometimes-obsessive thinking that comes with new love.

Adrenaline: A spike in adrenaline causes classic physical signs of infatuation, like a racing heart, shaky hands and blushing cheeks.

Love Sick

In the Middle Ages, lovesickness was considered a genuine medical condition.

Whether it stemmed from unrequited love or the anguish of heartbreak, the affliction was seen as a form of deep melancholy – serious enough to require treatment.

Prescribed remedies ranged from bed rest and sunlight to inhaling fresh air and soaking in baths infused with moistening plants such as water lilies and violets. Specific diets were also recommended, which were believed to rebalance the body and spirit – often including lamb, lettuce, eggs, fish and ripe fruits.

“I fell in love the way you fall asleep: slowly, and then all at once.”

JOHN GREEN,
THE FAULT IN OUR STARS, 2012

Third Time Lucky

Sixty-seven per cent of Americans reported having loved more than one person in their lifetime. The idea is echoed in the popular "Three Loves Theory", which suggests that we experience three different types of love at different stages in our lives – each teaching us something new.

The theory was first popularized in 2004 by relationship expert Helen Fisher, who argued that lust, passion and long-term commitment are separate experiences, each rooted in different parts of the brain. According to Fisher, love isn't a single feeling – it's a complex, evolving journey that reflects our growth, desires and emotional needs over time.

Lust

In our early lives we're likely to experience fairytale love – intense and all-consuming but primarily driven by physical attraction. Led by the brain's primitive, instinctive region, these romances are thrilling but often short-lived, rooted in desire rather than depth.

Passion

During the sexual awakening of our early twenties, we might fall into an intensely passionate romance – driven by the mammalian brain, which governs emotions and attachment. It's thrilling, dramatic and often a rollercoaster of highs and lows.

Commitment

As we mature, the rational brain takes the lead. Having learned from past relationships, we begin to prioritize emotional security, acceptance and the stability of long-term connection.

Love Is in the Air

Around one in 50 people have found love on an airplane* – that's according to over 2,000 travellers from Hong Kong to the United Arab Emirates.

This might be because a sense of adventure was rated one of the most attractive traits by 87 per cent of singles on the dating site match.com in 2017.

Spontaneity, travel and trying new things have also been linked to stronger long-term relationships, as they stimulate the brain's dopamine reward system – the same one activated by the euphoric feeling of falling in love.

Romantic Escapes

Travel is one of the most meaningful experiences you can share as a couple.

In 2024, *Time Out* compiled a list of the most romantic destinations in the world – and surprisingly, four regions outranked even Paris, the so-called "City of Love":

1. **Venice, Italy**
2. **Niagara Falls, Canada/USA**
3. **Marrakech, Morocco**
4. **Hoi An, Vietnam**
5. **Paris, France**
6. **Zanzibar, Tanzania**
7. **Prague, Czech Republic**
8. **Kyoto, Japan**
9. **Herzegovina**
10. **Montreal, Canada**

Wedding Bells

Christmas Eve
Christmas Day
New Year's Eve

The three most romantic days of the year all fall during the festive season.

Every year, a flurry of proposals take place between November and February, making the holidays the most popular time to pop the question.

24 July 2011

On this day, same-sex marriage became legal in the state of New York under the Marriage Equality Act – 823 same-sex couples received marriage licences and wed in New York City within the same 24 hours.

Almost one million same-sex marriages have taken place in the US since.

“I knew I loved you when 'home' went from being a place to being a person.”

POET AND AUTHOR ERIC MICHA'EL LEVENTHAL

Popping the Question

You might assume a once-in-a-lifetime trip is the perfect moment to propose – but for 49 per cent of Brits, home really is where the heart is.

More popular than a romantic dinner or a sunset on the beach, proposing to your partner in private, under your own roof, was the top choice in a 2016 poll by jeweller Beaverbrooks.

It's a different story in the US, where just over a third of proposals take place in scenic locations, and eight per cent take place while on holiday.

Love Languages

Marriage counsellor Dr Gary Chapman identified five distinct ways that people express and receive love – known as the Five Love Languages.

Understanding and "speaking" your partner's love language can strengthen emotional connection and deepen your relationship.

1. **Acts of Service:** Fixing problems and helping out is your way of supporting and showing up for someone.

2. **Gifts:** Tangible gestures are the most meaningful way to express your appreciation.

3. **Physical Touch:** Feeling physically connected to others through cuddling, stroking or holding hands strengthens your bonds.

4. **Quality Time:** You place importance on being together and sharing meaningful experiences.

5. **Words of Affirmation:** Encouragement and compliments, whether written or spoken out loud, make you feel confident, secure and loved.

Are Soulmates Real?

Every day, around three million first dates take place. But is there really such a thing as "the one"?

Science hasn't confirmed that yet – but research shows that long-term partners can become so emotionally and physically in sync, their hearts quite literally beat as one:

- **Heart rates of romantic partners can synchronize when they're near each other.**
- **Holding hands can align breathing patterns.**
- **Couples often develop similar facial expressions over time.**
- **Even body odour is more alike between close friends than between strangers.**

Qualities Women Love in a Man

(beyond good looks)

In September 2022, *Brides* wedding magazine revealed what women really want – and it turns out, looks aren't everything.

Counsellor and professor Dr Suzanne Degges-White shared the eight qualities that experts say heterosexual women are most drawn to in a partner. According to her, it's less about appearance and more about emotional connection, values and character:

- **Confidence**
- **Trustworthiness**
- **Integrity**
- **Compassion**
- **Emotional availability**
- **Respect**
- **Sense of humour**
- **Maturity**

"Shall I compare thee to a summer's day?
Thou art more lovely and more temperate.
Rough winds do shake the darling buds of May,
And summer's lease hath all too short a date.
Sometime too hot the eye of heaven shines,
And often is his gold complexion dimmed;
And every fair from fair sometime declines,
By chance, or nature's changing course, untrimmed;
But thy eternal summer shall not fade,
Nor lose possession of that fair thou ow'st,
Nor shall death brag thou wand'rest in his shade,
When in eternal lines to Time thou grow'st.
So long as men can breathe, or eyes can see,
So long lives this, and this gives life to thee."

WILLIAM SHAKESPEARE,
'SHALL I COMPARE THEE TO A SUMMER'S DAY
(SONNET 18)', 1609

My Everything

"The key to healthy aging is relationships, relationships, relationships,"

said psychiatrist George Vaillant, who spent over 30 years leading an 80-year Harvard study on long-term happiness.

Since 1938, researchers have tracked the lives of hundreds of participants and found that love – and the quality of close relationships – was the biggest predictor of lasting joy. In fact, those who were happiest in their relationships in their 50s turned out to be the healthiest in their 80s.

Chapter Two

Romantic Symbols

❤ Hearts

The love heart is the second-most-used emoji worldwide – and one of the most enduring and recognizable symbols of romance. But it's iconic shape may not actually come from the human heart, once believed to be the centre of emotion. Instead, some theories trace its origins to nature:

- ❤ **Ivy leaves, symbolizing fidelity in ancient Greece**
- ❤ **Seeds of the Silphium plant, a now-extinct herb prized in ancient Rome for its use as an aphrodisiac**

❤ The Colour Red

Red is the colour of roses, hearts, first-date lipsticks and Valentine's Day cards – but our association with it might be more primal than poetic.

Attraction literally makes the heart race, sending fresh blood rushing to the skin and creating that telltale rosy flush. Psychologists have found that simply seeing the colour red can raise your heart rate.

In one 2012 study, men rated women dressed in red as significantly more sexually attractive – suggesting that red doesn't just symbolize desire, it stimulates it.

❤ Cupid

In Roman mythology, Cupid was the symbol of desire and affection – a cherubic, winged matchmaker whose golden-tipped arrows could make anyone fall madly in love.

He was the Roman counterpart of the Greek god Eros, the embodiment of erotic love. As the son of Venus (goddess of love) and Mars (god of war), Cupid represented a powerful union of passion and conflict – an early inspiration for the age-old idea that *"love conquers all"*.

❤ Kamadeva

Kamadeva is the Hindu god of erotic love. His name comes from the word *kama*, meaning "sexual desire" (as in the famous *Kama Sutra*), and *deva*, meaning "deity".

Much like Cupid, Kamadeva is often depicted as a youthful, sometimes winged figure, who shoots love-laced arrows or darts to stir passion. In some of his earliest depictions, he is frequently shown alongside Rati, the great love of his life, who embodies female desire – making them a divine pair symbolizing the mutual nature of attraction.

❤ Harp

One of the most romantic instruments of all time, the harp is a popular choice for wedding ceremonies and emotional film scores. In Celtic culture, this ancient instrument symbolized the transcendental power of string music to move the soul. In Nordic mythology, its strings were seen as a ladder – a metaphor for ascending to higher states of love and connection. Even Cupid, when not holding his iconic bow and arrow, was also often portrayed holding a harp, further linking the instrument with themes of romance and desire.

“If music be the food of love, play on.”

WILLIAM SHAKESPEARE,
TWELFTH NIGHT, 1601–1602

❤ Swans

The way that swans curve their necks to form a heart shape has become a universal symbol of affection and tenderness. As graceful as they are devoted, swans are known to mate for life, often staying together for more than two decades. When a pair first bonds, they perform elegant dances, synchronize their movements and spend intentional time with each other – much like humans in love. When it comes to raising a family, they share responsibilities equally, protecting and nurturing their young as a united pair.

❤ Jasmine

Scents like Jasmine have long been intertwined with the idea of love. Known for its rich fragrance – especially potent at night – jasmine is believed to promote passion and sensuality. The flower's alluring scent is commonly found in women's perfumes, wedding bouquets and even traditional love spells. In Hinduism, jasmine holds deep symbolic meaning, representing beauty and attraction, and it is closely associated with the love goddess Kamadeva.

❤ Roses

In Greek mythology, the goddess of love, Aphrodite, is said to have named the rose after her son Eros – a poetic anagram of his name. One legend tells of Aphrodite rushing through a white rosebush to save her mortal love, Adonis, who was under attack. As she fought her way through the thorns, she cut her ankles, and her blood stained the white petals red. From then on, the red rose became a powerful symbol of eternal love and sacrifice.

❤ Aphrodite's Charms

The goddess of love was associated with many romantic symbols that we still recognize today:

Apples:
Forbidden love, temptation

Pomegranates:
Fertility, prosperity

Seashells:
Serenity, femininity, love

White doves:
Purity, loyalty, monogamy

Myrtles:
Quiet devotion, beauty, luck

❤ Claddagh Ring

Claddagh Rings have been crafted in Galway, Ireland, since at least the year 1700. Instantly recognizable, the design features a heart (symbolizing love) topped with a crown (for loyalty) and held between two hands (for friendship). Traditionally given as tokens of love or worn as engagement and wedding rings, Claddagh rings have deep roots in Irish culture. It wasn't until the nineteenth century that they gained popularity beyond the small fishing village they're named after – but notable wearers like Queen Victoria, John F. Kennedy and Walt Disney helped cement their place in global tradition.

❤ Diamonds

Engagement rings have symbolized love and commitment since ancient Rome, when rings were often crafted from iron to represent strength and permanence. However, the tradition of proposing with a precious stone – especially diamonds – didn't take hold until the 1930s. In the wake of the Great Depression, advertising campaigns promoted diamonds as "unbreakable" and "forever", linking their durability to the endurance of true love. These campaigns also implied that a man's devotion could be measured by the size and cost of the diamond he gave – a marketing idea that still lingers today.

❤ Celtic Love Knot

Before the exchange of rings became tradition, ancient lovers expressed their devotion through exchanging interwoven loops, known as Celtic Love Knots – or Anam Cara Knots. These endless loops, whether crafted in thread or precious metals, symbolized eternal bonds and unbreakable connection. Today, modern interpretations often feature interlocking hearts to represent two lives intertwined in unity and lasting love.

❤ Welsh Love Spoon

The tradition of gifting wooden "love spoons" has been alive in Wales for centuries. Traditionally carved by hand from a single piece of wood, they were once a suitor's way of impressing his future father-in-law – demonstrating both craftsmanship and commitment to his beloved. Today, love spoons are decorative in nature, often given as heartfelt gifts to couples celebrating weddings, anniversaries or other special milestones.

❤ Chocolate

Chocolate and romance go hand-in-hand – and there's science behind it. Eating chocolate sparks the same chemical euphoria as falling in love. That's because it contains phenylethylamine (PEA), a compound naturally released in the brain during moments of infatuation. PEA helps trigger the release of dopamine, the neurotransmitter associated with pleasure and reward. So, not only is chocolate a sweet gift for Valentine's Day, it may also enhance feelings of attraction.

Did you know?

The first heart-shaped box of chocolates was gifted on 14 February 1868. It was the invention of Richard Cadbury, heir to the Cadbury Chocolate empire, who created what he called a "fancy box" – an ornately decorated tray of rich chocolates arranged, for the first time, in the shape of a love heart. His romantic innovation transformed Valentine's Day gifting forever, establishing a tradition that still melts hearts today.

Signs of the Zodiac:
Most Compatible Love Matches

ARIES (21 March–19 April)
❤❤❤❤❤ **Aquarius**

TAURUS (20 April–20 May)
❤❤❤❤❤ **Capricorn**

GEMINI (21 May–20 June)
❤❤❤❤❤ **Sagittarius**

CANCER (21 June–22 July)
❤❤❤❤❤ **Scorpio**

LEO (23 July–22 August)
❤❤❤❤❤ **Libra**

VIRGO (23 August–22 September)
❤❤❤❤❤ **Pisces**

LIBRA (23 September–22 October)
❤❤❤❤❤ Leo

SCORPIO (23 October–21 November)
❤❤❤❤❤ Cancer

SAGITTARIUS (22 November–21 December)
❤❤❤❤❤ Gemini

CAPRICORN (22 December–19 January)
❤❤❤❤❤ Taurus

AQUARIUS (20 January–18 February)
❤❤❤❤❤ Aries

PISCES (19 February–20 March)
❤❤❤❤❤ Virgo

Chapter Three

Happily Ever After

In life, the best love stories don't have an ending. But when it comes to the stage, page and screen, we want nothing more than love, laughter and a

"happy ever after".

28 January 1813

America's favourite love story, *Pride & Prejudice*, was published in England on this date. Over 200 years later, Jane Austen's classic romantic novel was voted the nation's favourite book of all time in a poll spanning all 50 states*.

Written in an era when women were expected to secure marriages rather than careers, Jane Austen defied convention. Though she never married or had children herself, she called the novel – which she was forced to publish anonymously – her "darling child".

* America's 100 Favourite Books, Research by WordsRated, 31 January 2022

Fifty Shades of Grey

The bestselling romance series of all time is *Fifty Shades of Grey* (2011–2021) by E. L. James. The trilogy has sold over 150 million copies worldwide – more than five times as many as *Pride and Prejudice* (1813), which itself has sold an estimated 30 million copies over two centuries.

Romance remains the highest-earning genre in all of fiction.

Reading about romance makes us better at reading people.

One 2013 study found that readers of romance tend to be more attuned to social cues than fans of science fiction – suggesting that immersing yourself in love stories might sharpen emotional intelligence.

Surprisingly, a poll of American readers revealed that men actually read more romance than women. On average, women spent 52 fewer hours per year reading the genre compared to their male counterparts.

Between the Covers

When reading about love, most people image a familiar face – often their celebrity crush.

A 2025 study by Thrift Books found that 17 per cent of married readers picture their spouse as the love interest, while as many as seven per cent admitted to visualizing an ex instead.

Love Letters

Written declarations were once the currency of love – heartfelt letters sealed with ink before the digital age dulled the intimacy of saying "I love you".

Private exchanges, now made public, offer rare glimpses into some of history's most iconic relationships. In a letter to actress Marlene Dietrich, Ernest Hemingway confessed that being in her arms felt like "home". Even amid the demands of power, Napoleon Bonaparte wrote to his wife Joséphine de Beauharnais that he lived

"in the memory of [her] caresses".

These timeless words remind us that the most powerful love stories are often told in writing.

Did you know?

Outlaw Bonnie Parker cemented her place in history not just with a pistol, but with a pen – writing the prophetic poem 'The Story of Bonnie and Clyde'. Though Clyde Barrow was her most infamous partner in crime, he wasn't the only no-good man she was hopelessly devoted to. At the time of her death, Bonnie was still legally married to another man.

During a stint in jail, she would pass the time writing poetry and fantasizing about gangsters and doomed love affairs – a fascination that foreshadowed the tragic romance she would become most known for.

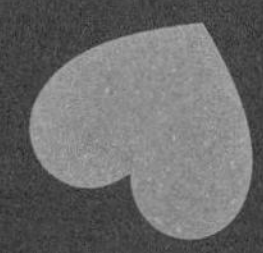

“Now if he returned
to me some time,
Tho he hadn’t a
penny to give,
I’d forget all this ‘hell’
he has caused me,
And love him as long
as I live.”

BONNIE PARKER,
‘THE STORY OF SUICIDE SAL’, 1932

Secret Love Letters of Oscar Wilde and Lord Alfred Douglas

Privately addressed to his lover, Lord Alfred Douglas, the now-famous letters of poet and playwright Oscar Wilde allowed the men to sustain their secret romance over the course of 11 years. In 1891, their love was forbidden – both socially and legally – and Wilde poured his affection, longing and anguish for Douglas into his words, sometimes writing from prison.

The letters not only capture the intensity of their relationship but also Wilde's deep frustration that the world could not, or would not, understand the depth of their love.

“Everyone is furious with me for going back to you, but they don’t understand us. I feel that it is only with you that I can do anything at all. Do remake my ruined life for me, and then our friendship and love will have a different meaning to the world. I wish that when we met at Rouen, we had not parted at all. There are such wide abysses now of space and land between us. But we love each other.”

OSCAR WILDE’S LOVE LETTER TO
LORD ALFRED DOUGLAS, AUGUST 1987

It's a Love Story

When it comes to romance films, most great stories follow one of seven classic themes – at least according to filmmaker community No Film School, which identified the most common narrative arcs used in cinema.

Love at first sight: Films like *500 Days of Summer* (2009) explore the spark of an instant romantic connection – that overwhelming feeling when two people seem destined to meet.

Opposites attract: This classic theme brings together star-crossed lovers from opposing worlds, like *Romeo + Juliet* (1996), where deep connection defies family, status or belief.

Second-chance romance: When love gets a do-over, the stakes are higher and the emotions are deeper – just like in *Casablanca* (1942).

Forbidden love: Films like *Brokeback Mountain* (2005) and *Call Me by Your Name* (2017) capture the tension, thrill and heartbreak of love that defies societal norms.

Love triangle: The classic dilemma of choosing between two suitors takes centre stage in *Bridget Jones's Diary* (2001), where audiences are split between the love interests.

Challenge and misunderstanding: Romantic misfires, mixed signals and unexpected hurdles drive the plot in *10 Things I Hate About You* (1999), a teen rom-com rooted in Shakespearean drama.

Happily ever after: Stories like *The Notebook* (2004) bring on the tears with soulmates who overcome time, obstacles and heartbreak to find lasting love.

Our Hearts Will Go On ... *and On*

Titanic, widely considered the greatest love story told on the big screen, was released 30 years ago. Premiering in 1997, the James Cameron epic became a cultural phenomenon, earning a staggering $2.26 billion (£1.64 billion) at the global box office. It remains the highest-grossing romantic film of all time.

Following its legacy, the *Twilight* series claims many of the top spots on the list of best-performing romantic films. Blending teen romance with supernatural drama, the saga captivated a generation and proved that star-crossed love stories still dominate the box office.

The Highest-Grossing Romantic Films

(After Titanic)

❤

Beauty and the Beast **(2017)**

$1.26 billion (£930 million)

Aladdin **(2019)**

$1.05 billion (£770 million)

The Twilight Saga:

Breaking Dawn - Part 2 **(2012)**

$848 million (£622 million)

The Twilight Saga:

Breaking Dawn - Part 1 **(2011)**

$712 million (£522 million)

Did you know?

You might know 'I Don't Want to Miss a Thing' as the epic love ballad from *Armageddon* (1998), performed by Aerosmith – but the song's real origin is far more intimate.

Songwriter Diane Warren was inspired by a 1997 interview with Barbra Streisand and her husband James Brolin. In the interview, Streisand recalled Brolin once telling her, "I don't want to fall asleep ... 'Cause then I'll miss you." The tender moment struck a chord with Warren, who later turned the line into the chorus of what would become one of the most iconic love songs in movie history.

Sexy Love

In June 2025, *New York Magazine*'s *The Cut* ranked the top sex scenes from mainstream movies. These were the best of the twenty-first century:

1. ***Atonement* (2007)**
2. ***Black Swan* (2010)**
3. ***The Notebook* (2004)**
4. ***Queen & Slim* (2019)**
5. ***Mr & Mrs Smith* (2005)**
6. ***Anna Karenina* (2012)**
7. ***Blue Valentine* (2010)**
8. ***Seven Pounds* (2008)**
9. ***Marie Antoinette* (2006)**
10. ***Revolutionary Road* (2008)**

Love on Set

In Hollywood, on-screen chemistry often spills over into real life – with many famous romances beginning on set, lasting long after the director calls "cut":

- **Zendaya and Tom Holland – *Spider-Man: Homecoming* (2017)**
- **Alicia Vikander and Michael Fassbender – *The Light Between Oceans* (2016)**
- **Ryan Gosling and Eva Mendes – *The Place Beyond the Pines* (2012)**
- **Natalie Portman and Benjamin Millepied – *Black Swan* (2010)**
- **Blake Lively and Ryan Reynolds – *Green Lantern* (2011)**
- **Freddie Prinze Jr. and Sarah Michelle Gellar – *I Know What You Did Last Summer* (1997)**

“If you live to be 100, I want to live to be 100 minus one day, so I never have to live without you.”

A.A. MILNE,
THE HOUSE AT POOH CORNER, 1928

Did you know?

The famous baseball player Joe DiMaggio sent fresh roses to Marilyn Monroe's grave three times a week for 20 years after she died.

Their passionate and often turbulent relationship has long been the subject of speculation, with some believing it played a role in her tragic downfall. Still, DiMaggio never remarried – and by many accounts, he loved her until the very end.

15 October 1839

On the day that Queen Victoria became engaged to the great love of her life, Prince Albert, she poured her joy into an elated diary entry:

"To feel I am loved by such an angel as Albert, is too great a happiness to describe, and I really felt it was the happiest and brightest moment in my life, which made up for all I had suffered and endured."

What followed was one of the most enduring love stories in British royal history. When Prince Albert died in 1861 at just 42 years old, Queen Victoria's grief was profound. She wore black every day for the rest of her life – a full four decades – in mourning for the man she called her soulmate.

Record-Breaking Love

From the three-day kiss to 86 years of marriage, these are the Guinness World Records that redefined

"couple goals".

Longest Kiss (2013)

58 hours, 35 minutes and 58 seconds

Longest Marriage (2011)

86 years, 9 months and 16 days

Longest Underwater Kiss (2010)

3 minutes and 24 seconds

Largest Underwater Wedding (2011)

303 guests

A Lifetime of Love

On average, humans will spend approximately 6.8 per cent of their lives simply enjoying the company of someone they love.

That adds up to roughly 1,769 days of dating, holidaying and domesticated bliss. In the grand timeline of life, love takes up more space than we might think.

Longest Celebrity Marriages

Dolly Parton and husband Carl Dean were married for 60 years when he died in 2025, making theirs one of the longest unions in showbusiness. These famous partnerships have stood the test of time:

45 years:

Samuel L. Jackson & LaTanya Richardson Jackson

37 years:

Tom Hanks & Rita Wilson

29 years:

Faith Hill & Tim McGraw

28 years:

Helen Mirren & Taylor Hackford

28 years:

Sarah Jessica Parker and Matthew Broderic

"Love has nothing to do with what you are expecting to get, only with what you are expecting to give – which is everything."

ACTRESS KATHARINE HEPBURN,
ME: STORIES OF MY LIFE, 1996

100 Million Ways to Say *"I Love You"*

Experts estimate that the number of love songs ever recorded has surpassed 100 million – a staggering testament to the power of love as a creative muse.

The oldest record of a love song dates all the way back to circa 2,000 BCE, titled 'The Love Song for Shu-Sin'. It celebrated not just romantic connection, but also erotic desire – proof that love has always stirred deep emotion.

Interestingly, research shows that men tend to sing about love more often than women, whether it's longing, heartbreak or passionate serenading. They're also, perhaps unsurprisingly, more likely to write lyrics about sex.

All You Need Is ...

Including the word "love" in a song title may be a secret formula for chart success. A staggering number of hit records share this trait – and some of music's most iconic acts prove it.

One fifth of the Beatles' bestselling singles featured the word "love" in the title, from 'All You Need Is Love' to 'She Loves You'.

The Supremes topped the chart six times using the word "love", while Whitney Houston achieved it four times – cementing "love" as one of the most commercially powerful words in music history.

According to UK music fans, Whitney Houston's 'I Will Always Love You' – released in 1992 – takes the crown as the most romantic song ever recorded.

The beloved ballad, featured in *The Bodyguard*, became an instant classic. It won multiple Grammy Awards, topped the charts around the world and was certified diamond in 2022 – a decade after Whitney's passing.

But here's a lesser-known fact: the song was originally written and recorded by country legend Dolly Parton in 1973 as a heartfelt farewell to her mentor and business partner Porter Wagoner. Whitney's soaring version gave it new life, but the original remains just as powerful.

First Dance Songs

The most requested and most romantic music at weddings is a mix of modern chart-toppers and classic love songs.

1. 'At Last', Etta James
2. 'Can't Help Falling in Love', Elvis Presley
3. 'Lover', Taylor Swift
4. 'Let's Stay Together', Al Green
5. 'Baby I'm Yours', Arctic Monkeys
6. 'Stand by Me', Ben E. King
7. 'This Will Be (An Everlasting Love)', Natalie Cole
8. 'Your Song', Elton John
9. 'All of Me', John Legend
10. 'I Won't Give Up', Jason Mraz

* Function Central UK findings from January 2025

In It for the Long Haul

Seahorses, swans, gibbons and eagles are just a few of the animal kingdom's most faithful lovers – known to choose one partner and stick with them for life.

Whie some species maintain multiple partners, 90 per cent of bird species and 3–5 per cent of mammals are considered monogamous. That means they pair up, raise their families together and care for one another – sometimes until the end.

Here are some of nature's most loyal creatures:

- ❤ **Wolves**
- ❤ **Beavers**
- ❤ **California Mice**
- ❤ **Anglerfish**
- ❤ **Black Vultures**
- ❤ **Prairie Voles**
- ❤ **Cockroaches**
- ❤ **Atlantic Puffin**

"Peacocking"

Dating in the animal kingdom is full of strange mating rituals, and a few of them seem quite romantic.

Robins bring females food during a period of courtship to strengthen them up for childbearing.

Adders massage a female's body with their tongue to encourage mating.

Black grouse fan out their tail feathers and flash their white plumage. It's called "lekking".

Frogs and toads are attracted to males with the longest and loudest croaks.

Female glow-worms light up all over to grab the attention of a male suitor.

Chapter Four

Self-Love

“Self-love, my liege, is not so vile a sin, as self-neglecting.”

A. A. MILNE,
THE HOUSE AT POOH CORNER, 1928

Fill Your Own Cup First

There's a reason why they say: put on your own life jacket first. In love, just like in life, caring for yourself isn't selfish – it's essential. Learning how to love yourself is the foundation for trusting, supporting and loving someone else.

Self-love means recognizing that how you treat yourself sets the tone for every other relationship in your life. It's about showing up for your needs, respecting your boundaries and knowing your worth.

Because once your own cup is full, you'll have more to give.

Self-Love in Chinese Culture

Self-love is a fundamental part of Chinese culture. Where Western ideals of loving yourself often value taking care and building self-esteem, Chinese culture considers a sense of "self" as an extension of your place in the family and society.

Restraint

Following societal expectations and refraining from bad behaviours (such as cheating or drug use) means self-respect.

Responsibility

When you abide by a set of core values, such as doing your best and taking care of your family, you set high standards for yourself.

Persistence

Respect others but have independence and adherence to your own thoughts and ideas, which will not be compromised.

Cherishing

Valuing your life and body as highly as your property and possessions helps you to protect and take care of them.

Acceptance

Being at peace with your past self, and finding satisfaction with your present, is a conscious part of living a harmonious life.

"I must undertake to love myself and to respect myself as though my very life depends upon self-love and self-respect."

AMERICAN POET JUNE JORDAN,
BLACK WOMEN WRITERS AND FEMINISM PANEL,
1978

Heal Your Own Heart

Having compassion for yourself can keep your heart healthy. Research among 195 women (aged around 59) showed that those who treated themselves with more kindness and understanding had thinner carotid artery walls and less plaque build-up in the heart.

Overall, the University of Pittsburgh study (2021) found that greater self-compassion was associated with lower subclinical cardiovascular disease.

Love Yourself: Act #1

People who regularly show greater levels of gratitude have higher self-esteem and better wellbeing. That's what a study of 235 Chinese undergraduates found in 2015. It's also been shown numerous times that higher self-esteem is a predictor of stronger romantic relationships. Luckily, gratitude is a construct we all control. From saying it out loud to quiet contemplation or writing down a physical list, there are plenty of ways to show gratitude in everyday life.

“If you can’t love yourself, how in the hell are you gonna love somebody else?”

RUPAUL CHARLES,
RUPAUL'S DRAG RACE

10 Things to Be Grateful For

Gratitude is one of the simplest ways to shift your mindset and lift your mood. Whether you're having the best day or a difficult one, taking a moment to reflect on the good can bring comfort, clarity and calm. Here are ten everyday things to be thankful for:

1. **A warm bed – a safe, soft place to rest is a luxury not everyone has.**
2. **Loved ones – family, chosen family, friends or even a kind stranger can make all the difference.**
3. **Your body – for all it does: carrying you, healing you and letting you experience the world.**
4. **Laughter – a giggle, a belly laugh or a joyful memory that still makes you smile.**

5. **Nature** – trees, sunshine, fresh air, or a quiet moment watching the clouds.
6. **Clean water** – easy to overlook, but essential and life-giving.
7. **Moments of peace** – that stillness between the chaos where you can just breathe.
8. **Music** – songs that move you, lift you, or say the things you can't express.
9. **Learning** – every mistake or lesson shapes the person you're becoming.
10. **Today** – a brand new chance to start again, to try something new, or simply be.

No matter how small, recognizing the good helps you notice more of it. Gratitude isn't about pretending everything is perfect – it's about finding light, even in the cracks.

Did you know?

There's nothing humans love to talk about more, than themselves.

Science says that sharing information about ourselves activates the same reward centres in the brain as eating good food, taking drugs and even having sex.

So, make your specialist

subject: *you*.

“Her life with others no longer interests him. He wants only her stalking beauty, her theatre of expressions. He wants the minute secret reflection between them, the depth of field minimal, their foreignness intimate like two pages of a closed book.”

MICHAEL ONDAATJE,
THE ENGLISH PATIENT, 1992

Films About Learning to Love Yourself

Turn on a feel-good film and fall in love with someone else's self-discovery story.

1. *Little Miss Sunshine* (2006)
2. *Moonlight* (2016)
3. *Funny Girl* (1968)
4. *Hairspray* (2007)
5. *Muriel's Wedding* (1994)
6. *Soul* (2020)
7. *Eat Pray Love* (2010)
8. *Wild* (2014)
9. *Yes Man* (2008)
10. *The Perks of Being a Wallflower* (2012)

Great sleep = *higher self-worth*

Sleeping the optimal eight hours every night can boost your self-esteem and sense of self-worth.

Researchers in the US proved that sleep deprivation (under six hours) limited feelings of optimism in 1,805 adults almost as much as getting too much sleep (over nine hours).

Loving your sleep therefore means loving yourself.

Love Yourself: Act #2

According to research conducted by Canada's Queen's University in 2020, of the 6,200 thoughts humans have every day, around 80 per cent of them are negative. The study even showed that these negative thoughts feed through to our cells and put stress on the body.

Therefore, the importance of speaking positively to yourself can't be overstated. It starts with paying yourself compliments (such as, *my eyes are an interesting colour, or my hair looks good today*) – the same things you would tell a loved one.

“Your self-worth is determined by you. You don’t have to depend on someone telling you who you are.”

BEYONCÉ
ON CONFIDENCE AND SELF-LOVE
FOR *GQ*, JANUARY 2013

10 Things I Love About Myself

Self-love isn't always easy – but it's powerful. Taking time to reflect on the qualities that make you who you are can help build confidence, resilience and inner peace. Here's a list to get you started, but feel free to make it your own:

1. **My strength – I've been through challenges and come out stronger each time.**
2. **My kindness – I care deeply, and I show up for the people I love.**
3. **My sense of humour – I can laugh at life and sometimes even at myself.**
4. **My creativity – I have ideas that no one else does, and I bring them to life in my own way.**

5. **My intuition** – I trust my gut, and it's often right.
6. **My curiosity** – I'm always learning, growing, and asking questions.
7. **My resilience** – Even when things don't go my way, I keep going.
8. **My heart** – I love deeply, fiercely and honestly.
9. **My uniqueness** – There's no one else like me, and that's my superpower.
10. **My progress** – I may not be where I want to be yet, but I'm proud of how far I've come.

Loving yourself is a journey – not a destination. Celebrate every step.

“Self-love is the source of all our other loves.”

YUNG PUEBLO

Main Character Energy

The great filmmaker Nora Ephron once said: "Above all, be the heroine of your life, not the victim."

Seeing your story this way gives you agency over your own destiny, instead of letting the plot happen to you. When you place greatest importance on yourself, as the protagonist, the direction seems clearer – and better yet, more exciting.

Mindset Swaps

Sometimes the words in your head need a more loving spin.

ENVY → INSPIRATION

REGRET → GROWTH

STAGNANT → BREATHING SPACE

NO → NOT RIGHT NOW

UNFAIR → NOT MEANT TO BE

“If you’re not someone who has a natural and effortless love for yourself, it’s hard to let go of your desire to please other people, and that’s really not an ingredient for a happy life.”

ANNE HATHAWAY,
NEW YORK TIMES MAGAZINE, JANUARY 2015

Go Solo

No date? No problem. Don't miss out on the things you love just because you're going it alone.

Cinema: **Sink into the story without distractions – find magic in enjoying your own company.**

Dinner: **Savour every bite, order exactly what you love and finish the dessert all by yourself.**

Road trip: **Total freedom – your playlist, your snacks, your pace. The open road never felt so good.**

Hiking: **Reconnect with yourself and nature, one mindful step at a time.**

Theatre: **Say yes to spontaneous shows and score great seats – no need to coordinate with anyone else.**

Love Yourself: Act #3

Around half of Brits have never received a love letter, even though a third of them say it's the ultimate romantic gesture.

For the writer, connecting the hand movement with the brain's deep and conscious loving thoughts is said to release dopamine – not forgetting the reward it gives the reader. So, imagine being the giver and receiver of a letter dedicated entirely to you. The pleasure is all yours.

“Where there is love there is life”

MAHATMA GANDHI
(1869–1943)